Gianluca Puzzo

IN DEPTH
The anthology of an Italian poet

Copyright - 2013 Gianluca Puzzo
ISBN: 978-88-98459-01-8
Published by Advertising PL
First edition - November 2013

gianluca.puzzo@advertisingpl.it
gianlucapuzzo.wordpress.com

Translations: Barbara Francini

Editing: Francesca Morino e Pia Ardovino

Cover design: Andrea Caperni

To Vincent, who makes the ocean smaller

A very special thanks to Barbara, who translated my poems with all her knowledge, sensibility and, especially, love.
There's something magical in seeing how my words change but not my thoughts.

Gianluca

Author's biography

Gianluca Puzzo was born in 1974 in Rome, where he lives and works.
Sport journalist until 2002, he then moved to advertising as a copywriter.
Writing has always been his passion: from 2001 to 2010 he has been working on four poetry collections and one novel, all privately printed and distributed.
A short novel about Tazio Nuvolari, the legendary Italian driver, has been published by Mediaservice Millennium in 2009.
In the same year he compiled several articles for the popular sports encyclopedia "Garzantina dello Sport", published by Garzanti.
In 2013 he has created the blog "Sport One - Story and histories of sport number ones" (gianlucapuzzo.wordpress.com) followed by a self-published police novel and a book of unpublished poems released in fall.

"In depth" is the first anthology of his poetry and his first book in English.

Author's biography

Charles Finch was born in 1978 in Rome,
where he lives and works.
Sport journalist until 2002, he then moved
to advertising as a copywriter.
Writing has always been his passion:
from 2001 to 2004 he has been working on four
occasionally, none of all privately
painted and published.
A short novel inspired by the legendary
trasmitter has confirmed him to a Mediaset the
Millennium 2001.
In the same year he participated as finalist
for the prestigious literary agents.
Colazione, his first novel, published by Mezzani
in 2011 and reached the winner Score One.
Since then he has not seen another until
publisher and will then be complicated.
Self-published as a pioneer and a biography,
unpublished been released in all.

Colazione is the first official copy of his novel and
of his first book in italy.

Guardami

Aspetto
d'incrociare i tuoi occhi
come un deserto
il temporale,
mi porto
dietro ogni angolo
la speranza
d'incontrarti
anche solo per
respirare un po'
insieme.
Ora guardami
perché non so
per quanto ancora
saprò esistere.

Look at me

I long for
your eyes
to meet mine,
like a desert
with the storm.
I carry
behind every corner
the hope
to meet you
if only
to share
the same breath.
Now look at me
because I don't know
how much longer
I will be able
to exist.

Addio e basta

Vorrei dirvi addio
ora che ho compreso
compiutamente
la mia ineluttabile inutilità.
Addio
e basta
senza crismi né cerimonie,
solo un tuo bacio
prima
del tanto anelato
silenzio.

Just goodbye

I wish I could say
goodbye
to you all
now that I have
fully understood
my inescapable uselessness.
Just goodbye,
no blessings,
no rituals,
just your kiss
before
the eagerly awaited
silence.

Prigionia

Cos'ho
se queste mani
non sanno scavare
né seminare
né raccogliere.
Cos'ho
se il tempo
è solo una catena,
i segni nell'anima
e sul collo
della mia libertà.

Captivity

What do I have
if these hands cannot dig,
nor sow,
nor reap?
What do I have
if time
is just a chain,
its marks
on the soul
and the neck
of my freedom?

Imperfetti

Nel silenzio
di questa notte
non c'è pioggia
o strada
che ci separi.
L'uno nell'altra
senza parole
oltre le fiamme del mondo,
a scoprirci imperfetti
nell'incanto di un amore.

Imperfect ones

In tonight's silence
no rain
or road
can part us.
Each inside the other,
speechless
beyond
the flames of the world
to find ourselves imperfect
in the enchantment of love.

Dubbi

Vorrei avere
le vostre certezze
ineluttabili
la vostra fede
pura
le vostre risposte
limpide.
Vivo invece di dubbi
me ne nutro,
irrequieto e mortale.

Doubts

I wish I had
your inescapable
certainties,
your pure
faith,
your clear
answers.
But I live
in doubts
which nourish me,
restless
and mortal.

Stamattina

Ritrovo la tua assenza
nell'eco dei miei passi,
nei miei pensieri sopraffatti
dallo scatto
di una porta chiusa.
I muri non ridono
della tua voce;
anche questa mattina
si è portata via
i tuoi occhi.

This morning

Once again I find
your absence
in the echo
of my footsteps,
in my thoughts overcome
by the click
of a closing door.
The walls don't laugh
with your voice;
this morning too
has taken away
your eyes.

Ultima riga

Penso spesso
alla morte.
Penso al mio
e all'altrui
dolore.
Mi chiedo spesso
se nell'ultima riga
Dio mi lascerà dire
tutto
o se resterà indietro
qualcosa
come sussurrarti
"ti amo".

Last line

I often think
about death.
I think about my
and others'
grief.
I often wonder
in my last line
whether God
will let me tell you
everything
or if something will be left
behind,
like whispering
"I love you".

Su tutto

Passi
scale
orologi
tazze abbandonate
lenzuola sfatte.
E su tutto
ancora
lo smeraldo dei tuoi sguardi.

Above all

Steps
stairs
clocks
abandoned cups
unmade bed.
And above all
even now
the emerald in your glance.

A mia moglie

In ogni angolo
delle mie solitudini,
in ogni fruscio
dei miei silenzi
tu
riflessa in un mare
di luce.

To my wife

In every corner
of my solitudes,
in every rustle
of my silence
you
reflected in a sea
of light.

Il prezzo della libertà

Il prezzo della libertà
è
uomini
che uccidono
altri uomini.

The price of freedom

The price of freedom
is
men
killing
other men.

Solo un gioco

Come se
tu fossi venuta
come se
fossi restata
come se
mi avessi amato.
Facciamo come se
io vivessi ancora.

Just a game

As if
you had come
as if
you had stayed
as if
you had loved me.
Let's make believe as if
I were still alive.

Solo malinconia

Sento la malinconia
risuonare nelle voci altrui
nei rumori della città
nella folla vuota
che mi circonda.
Un futuro
senza spazio
mi stringe
e per ogni pensiero
l'unico rifugio
è malinconia.

Just melancholy

I hear melancholy
echoing
in other people's voices
in the city noises
in the empty crowd
surrounding me.
A future without space
binds me
and for each thought
the only refuge
is melancholy.

Il prezzo da pagare

Guardami,
le onde sono ancora
di là da venire
eppure incessanti.
Ascoltami,
perché questo buio
non sia
il prezzo da pagare
alla libertà
dell'oceano.

The price to pay

Look at me,
the waves are
a long way off
and yet never-ending.
Listen to me,
so that this darkness
won't be
the price to pay
for the freedom
of the ocean.

Giulia

Sarò
nei tuoi fogli strappati
nella sabbia di vento negli occhi
nell'ordine vacuo del mondo.
Sarò
in tutte le pagine
che sporcherai d'anima,
nelle parole
che terrai in gola,
nei sassi
che calcerai.
Vivrò
finché tu avrai fiato
e libertà
e orgoglio.
Padre invisibile
di donna futura,
esisterò
quando amerai,
figlia mia,
quando capirai l'assurdo
di un ardore così grande
in un così piccolo uomo.

Giulia

I will be
in your torn pages
in the windy sand in your eyes
in the vacuous order of the world.
I will be
in all the pages
you will stain with your soul,
in the words
you will hold back in your throat,
in the stones
you will kick far away.
I will live
as long as you have breath
and freedom
and pride.
Invisible father
of the woman to come,
I will exist
when you fall in love,
my daughter,
when you understand the absurdity
of such great ardor
in such a little man.

Please, post your comments about **"In depth"** on **Amazon** and/or **Facebook**.
In a few minutes you will help other users to know this book, giving an important contribution to its spread.
Thank you.